Madonna Quiz Book

101 Questions To Test Your Knowledge
Of This Incredibly Successful Musician

By Colin Carter
Published by Glowworm Press

Madonna Quiz

This book contains one hundred and one informative and entertaining trivia questions with multiple choice answers. With 101 questions, some easy, some more demanding, this entertaining book will really test your knowledge of the sensation that is Madonna.

You will be quizzed on a wide range of topics associated with Madonna for you to test yourself; with questions on her early days, her songs, her lyrics, her achievements, her awards, her charity work and much more, guaranteeing you a truly educational experience. The Madonna Quiz Book will provide entertainment for people of all ages and will certainly test your knowledge of this world famous superstar. The book is packed with information and is a must-have for all true Madonna fans, wherever you live in the world.

Disclaimer
All Rights Reserved. No part of this publication may be reproduced without the written permission of the publisher; with the exception of reviews written for a blog, website, magazine or newspaper. Product names referred to within this publication are the property of their respective trademark holders. This book is unofficial and is not authorised by the aforementioned interests. This book is licensed for your personal enjoyment only.

FOREWORD

When I was asked to write a foreword to this book I was incredibly flattered.

I have known Colin for a number of years and his knowledge of facts and figures is phenomenal.

His love for music and his talent for writing quiz books makes him the ideal man to pay homage to the true genius that is Madonna.

This book came about as a result of a challenge over a beer or two!

I do hope you enjoy the book.

Dave Bunty

Here goes with the first block of questions.

1. What was Madonna born as?
    A. Madonna Lacey Ciccone
    B. Madonna Lisa Ciccone
    C. Madonna Louise Ciccone
    D. Madonna Lucinda Ciccone

2. When was she born?
    A. 1955
    B. 1956
    C. 1957
    D. 1958

3. Where was Madonna born?
    A. Michigan
    B. Minnesota
    C. Missouri
    D. Montana

4. How tall is Madonna?
    A. 5 feet 4 inches
    B. 5 feet 5 inches
    C. 5 feet 6 inches
    D. 5 feet 7 inches

5. What is her Catholic confirmation name?
    A. Danica
    B. Jannica
    C. Monica

    D. Veronica

6. What is the name of Madonna's first child?
    A. Carlos
    B. Lourdes
    C. Mercy
    D. Rocco

7. How many children does Madonna have?
    A. 4
    B. 5
    C. 6
    D. 7

8. What is the name of Madonna's first husband?
    A. Sean Bean
    B. Sean Connery
    C. Sean Hannity
    D. Sean Penn

9. What is the name of Madonna's second husband?
    A. Ritchie Blackmore
    B. Richie Sambora
    C. Guy Fawkes
    D. Guy Ritchie

10. What is Madonna often referred to as?
    A. Countess of Pop
    B. Duchess of Pop
    C. Empress of Pop

D. Queen of Pop

OK, so here are the answers to the first ten questions. If you get seven or more right, you are doing very well so far, but the questions will get harder.

A1. Madonna was born as Madonna Louise Ciccone.

A2. Madonna was born on 16th August 1958. The Zodiac sign for her date of birth makes her a Leo.

A3. Madonna was born in Bay City in Michigan. Madonna referred to her birthplace as "a little, smelly town in Northern Michigan". As a piece of trivia, The Bay City Rollers, a hugely popular band in the 1970s, were named after the lead singer randomly threw a dart at a map and it landed on Bay City.

A4. Madonna revealed in Star Hits magazine in 1984 that she was 5 feet 4inches tall saying, "I always wanted to be taller. I feel like a shrimp, but that's the way it goes".

A5. Madonna was confirmed in the Catholic Church in 1966, when she was given Veronica as her confirmation name.

A6. Madonna's first child was a daughter named Lourdes Maria Ciccone Leon who was born in 1996. Her father is actor Carlos Leon.

A7. Madonna has six children. In addition to her two biological children, Lourdes and Rocco, she has four children she adopted from Malawi on three separate occasions.

A8. Madonna married actor Sean Penn on her birthday in 1985, aged 27 years old. The marriage did not last long. After initially filing for an annulment in December 1987, Madonna filed for divorce in January 1989, citing irreconcilable differences.

A9. Madonna married her second husband Guy Ritchie at Skibo Castle in Scotland on 22nd December 2000.

A10. Madonna is often referred to as the Queen of Pop.

OK, back to the questions.

11. Where did Madonna work when she first moved to New York City?
    A. Bloomindales
    B. Burger King
    C. Dunkin Donuts
    D. Hooters

12. What was the name of Madonna's first band?
    A. Book Club
    B. Breakfast Club
    C. Country Club
    D. Culture Club

13. What was the name of Madonna's debut single?
    A. Borderline
    B. Burning Up
    C. Everybody
    D. Physical Attraction

14. What was the name of Madonna's debut album?
    A. A To Madonna
    B. Like A Virgin
    C. Madonna
    D. This is Madonna

15. What was Madonna's first number one single in the US?
    A. Dress You Up

    B. Like a Virgin
    C. Material Girl
    D. True Blue

16. What was Madonna's first single to make the charts in the UK?
    A. Borderline
    B. Holiday
    C. Lucky Star
    D. Material Girl

17. What was Madonna's first number one single in the UK?
    A. Borderline
    B. Crazy For You
    C. Into The Groove
    D. Papa Don't Preach

18. Where was Sire Records President Seymour Stein when he met Madonna?
    A. In a hospital
    B. In a hotel
    C. In jail
    D. In rehab

19. Which one-hit wonder did she support as a backing dancer in her first trip to Europe?
    A. Baccara
    B. Lipps, Inc.
    C. Ottawan

D. Patrick Hernandez

20. What is the official website address?
    A. Mad.com
    B. Madonna.com
    C. Madonnaonline.com
    D. OfficialMadonna.com

Here are the answers to the last set of questions.

A11. Long before she became the Queen of Pop, Madonna worked at Dunkin' Donuts in Times Square in New York City. She didn't work there for long as she admitted, "I was sacked for squirting donut jelly all over the customers."

A12. Madonna joined Breakfast Club, her first band, in 1979.

A13. Madonna's debut single was called Everybody which was released on 6th October 1982. It was not a commercial success.

A14. Madonna released her debut album entitled Madonna on 27th July 1983. Five singles were released from the album including the hits 'Holiday', 'Lucky Star', and 'Borderline'.

A15. The first number one single that Madonna had in the US wasn't until 1984 when 'Like a Virgin' topped the charts. As a bit of trivia Weird Al Jankovic recorded a parody version in 1985 entitled 'Lie A Surgeon'.

A16. 'Holiday' was Madonna's first single to chart in the UK, charting in January 1984. It is a song she often sings as part of her encore at live concerts.

A17. The first number one single that Madonna had in the UK wasn't until her eighth single released in the UK, when 'Into The Groove' topped the charts in August 1985 and stayed at the top for a total of four weeks.

A18. Stein was in hospital when he met Madonna and agreed to her first record contract. Sire Records signed an incredible range of artists including Depeche Mode, Echo & the Bunnymen, K.D. Lang, The Cure, The Pretenders, The Ramones, The Smiths, Seal, Soft Cell and Talking Heads amongst others.

A19. Madonna was a backing dancer to Patrick Hernandez in 1979. The French singer had a huge hit with a Euro pop song called 'Born to be alive'.

A20. Madonna.com is the official website. It provides a wealth of information including all the latest news, historical material and a complete discography.

Here goes with the next set of questions.

21. What song did Madonna open with at the 1985 Live Aid concert?
    A. Angel
    B. Holiday
    C. Into The Groove
    D. Open Your Heart

22. What band did Madonna play tambourine for at the 1985 Live Aid concert?
    A. Duran Duran
    B. Heaven 17
    C. Spandau Ballet
    D. Thompson Twins

23. Which model appeared in Madonna's controversial 1992 book 'Sex'?
    A. Carla Bruni
    B. Naomi Campbell
    C. Cindy Crawford
    D. Kate Moss

24. What song featured mermaids in the accompanying music video?
    A. Cherish
    B. Deeper And Deeper
    C. Express Yourself
    D. You Can Dance

25. What was the documentary 'Truth or Dare' known as internationally?
    A. Barely Madonna
    B. In Bed With Madonna
    C. Madonna Uncovered
    D. Twist or Stick

26. Who plays the part of Madonna's guardian angel in the music video to 'Bad Girl'?
    A. Bill Murray
    B. Jack Nicholson
    C. Christopher Walken
    D. Bruce Willis

27. When was Madonna indicted into the Rock and Roll Hall of Fame?
    A. 1992
    B. 1994
    C. 1996
    D. 1998

28. Who were Madonna's long time backing singers?
    A. Niki Haris and Donna De Loitte
    B. Niki Haris and Donna De Lorenzo
    C. Niki Haris and Donna De Lory
    D. Niki Haris and Donna De Lorean

29. What song features the lyrics "You're just jealous cause you can't be me"?

    A. Dress You Up
    B. Gambler
    C. Live To Tell
    D. Papa Don't Preach

30. What was the album that followed Like A Virgin?
    A. Bedtime Stories
    B. Erotica
    C. Like A Prayer
    D. True Blue

Here are the answers to the last set of questions.

A21. Madonna performed at Live Aid in front of 89,000 people in the JFK Stadium, Philadelphia USA on 13th July, 1985. She entered the stage at 4:27pm and started with 'Holiday' and she also performed 'Into The Groove' and finished her set with 'Love Makes The World Go Round'.

A22. Madonna played tambourine and sang backing vocals to The Thompson Twins at Live Aid. The Live Aid concerts was one of the largest television broadcasts of all time, with the concerts being seen by an estimated 40% of the global population. The event was organised by Sir Bob Geldof and Midge Ure to raise funds for the Ethiopian famine disaster.

A23. Supermodel Naomi Campbell appeared in an explicit scene alongside Madonna in the controversial coffee table-book 'Sex'. Also featuring in the book were actress Isabella Rossellini and rapper Vanilla Ice.

A24. Mermaids were featured in the music video for Madonna's 1989 hit Cherish. The video for the song was filmed at Paradise Cove Beach in Malibu, California and was directed by photographer Herb Ritts.

A25. Truth or Dare was a documentary film chronicling Madonna during her 1990 Blond Ambition Tour. It was known as In Bed with Madonna internationally.

A26. Christopher Walken plays the part of Madonna's guardian angel in the video to the 1993 single 'Bad Girl'.

A27. Madonna was indicted into the Rock and Roll Hall of Fame on 17th January 1996 in a ceremony at New York's Waldorf-Astoria Hotel.

A28. Niki Harris and Donna De Lory were the long term backing vocalists to Madonna. De Lory accompanied Madonna as a backing vocalist on every concert tour from 1987's Who's That Girl World Tour to 2006's Confessions Tour.

A29. 'Gambler' features the lyrics "You're just jealous cause you can't be me". The song was written solely by Madonna and it was used on the soundtrack to the 1985 film Vision Quest.

A30. Released in June 1986, 'True Blue' was the album released after 'Like A Virgin'.

Here is the next set of questions.

31. What song had the same name that was recorded twice with a completely different tune and lyrics?
    A. Forbidden Love
    B. Living For Love
    C. Runaway Love
    D. The Look Of Love

32. Which song includes the line 'Feels so good inside when you hold me'?
    A. Deeper And Deeper
    B. Express Yourself
    C. Justify My Love
    D. Like A Virgin

33. Which album did Prince work alongside Madonna as producer?
    A. Bedtime Stories
    B. Erotica
    C. Like a Prayer
    D. Something to Remember

34. What song did Lenny Kravitz write for Madonna?
    A. Erotica
    B. Express Yourself
    C. Hanky Panky
    D. Justify My Love

35. What was the most successful song from the True Blue album?
- A. La Isla Bonita
- B. Open Your Heart
- C. Papa Don't Preach
- D. True Blue

36. What song did Madonna open with at the 2005 Live 8 concert in London?
- A. Frozen
- B. La Isla Bonita
- C. Like A Prayer
- D. Vogue

37. What was the title of Madonna's first greatest hits album?
- A. The Immaculate Collection
- B. The Immaculate Conception
- C. The Immaculate Machine
- D. The Immaculate Reception

38. What was the title of Madonna's second greatest hits album?
- A. Complete Collection II
- B. GHV2
- C. The Hits Volume Two
- D. Ultimate Collection

39. Who wrote the song 'Bedtime Story'?

- A. Adele
- B. Bjork
- C. Kate Bush
- D. P J Harvey

40. Which country does Madonna hold the record for most number one singles by a female artist?
    - A. Australia
    - B. Canada
    - C. Spain
    - D. United Kingdom

Here are the answers to the last block of questions.

A31. Forbidden Love was a track on the 1994 album Bedtime Stories. A completely different song also called Forbidden Love was a track on the 2005 album Confessions on a Dance Floor.

A32. The lyric 'Feels so good inside when you hold me, and your heart beats and you love me' comes from her worldwide hit single 'Like A Virgin'.

A33. Prince collaborated with Madonna on the production of the 'Like a Prayer' album, part of which was recorded at Prince's Paisley Park studio in Minneapolis.

A34. Lenny Kravitz wrote 'Justify My Love' for Madonna in 1990.

A35. Five singles were released from the True Blue album. They were La Isla Bonita, Live to Tell, Open Your Heart, Papa Don't Preach and True Blue. Papa Don't Preach is widely recognised as being the most successful song from the album.

A36. Madonna opened her set at Live 8 with "Like A Prayer". She was dressed in all-white as were her backing singers The London Community Gospel Choir which made for a truly memorable sight. The other songs she performed to rapturous applause were "Ray of Light" and "Music".

A37. The Ultimate Collection was the title of Madonna's first greatest hits album. It was released in November 1990 and has gone on to sell over 30 million copies, which has made it the best selling compilation album by a solo artist of all time.

A38. Madonna's second greatest hits album was called GHV2 – which was an abbreviation of Greatest Hits Volume 2. The album includes songs that Madonna released between 1992 and 2001.

A39. Bjork wrote 'Bedtime Story'. It featured on the 1994 album 'Bedtime Stories'.

A40. Madonna holds the record for most number one singles by a female artist in Australia, Canada, Italy, Spain and the UK! Give yourself a bonus point if you knew that.

I hope you're learning some new facts about Madonna, and here is the next set of questions.

41. What entertainment company did Madonna form in 1992?
    A. Bohemian
    B. Maverick
    C. Outsider
    D. Unorthodox

42. Who became their best selling artist?
    A. Tori Amos
    B. Sheryl Crow
    C. Natalie Imbruglia
    D. Alanis Morissette

43. How many Grammy awards has Madonna won?
    A. 4
    B. 5
    C. 6
    D. 7

44. When did she win her first Grammy award?
    A. 1987
    B. 1989
    C. 1991
    D. 1993

45. Which of these is a popular Madonna tribute act?

    A. Always Madonna
    B. Counterfeit Madonna
    C. Miss Madonna
    D. Ultimate Madonna

46. Which song includes the line 'I do yoga and pilates and the room is full of hotties'?
    A. American Life
    B. Beautiful Life
    C. Love Life
    D. Sporting Life

47. What movie did Madonna act in that contained the famous line, "There's no crying in baseball"?
    A. A League Of Their Own
    B. Bull Durham
    C. Field of Dreams
    D. Major League

48. Which year did Madonna perform the half time show at the Super Bowl?
    A. 2010
    B. 2012
    C. 2014
    D. 2016

49. What foreign language was sung in 'Who's That Girl'?
    A. French
    B. German

C. Italian
D. Spanish

50. What drink brand used 'Like A Prayer' in its advertising campaign, prior to the song's release?
    A. Coca Cola
    B. Dr. Pepper
    C. Pepsi
    D. Sprite

Here are the answers to the last set of questions.

A41. Madonna formed Maverick in 1992 and it included a record label and a film production company. Its name was constructed from the names of **Ma**donna, **Ve**ronica and Frede**rick,** three of the company's founders.

A42. Maverick signed Canadian musician Alanis Morissette in 1994 and her first album with Maverick entitled Jagged Little Pill was released in 1995. This album achieved overall global sales of 33 million units making it the best selling album in the label's history.

A43. Madonna has won a total of seven Grammy awards.

A44. Madonna won her first Grammy award in 1991 for 'Best Music Video, Long Form' for 'Madonna – Blond Ambition World Tour Live'.

A45. There are a number of Madonna tribute acts, but perhaps the best known is Miss Madonna. Other tribute acts include Material Girl and Vogue Madonna.

A46. The lyric 'I do yoga and pilates and the room is full of hotties' comes from her 2003 single 'American Life'.

A47. "There's no crying in baseball" was a famous line uttered by Tom Hanks in the 1992 movie 'A League Of Their Own'. As well as Madonna, the movie also starred Geena Davis. Madonna recorded 'This Used to Be My Playground' as the theme to the film, and it featured over the closing credits.

A48. On 5th February 2012 Madonna performed at the Super Bowl XLVI halftime show at the Lucas Oil Stadium in Indianapolis. It is one of the most spectacular shows ever seen at a Super Bowl and was watched by an estimated 115 million viewers.

A49. 'Who's That Girl' featured Spanish lyrics. The song included these lines "Quien es esa nina, who's that girl. Senorita, mas fina, who's that girl". Her previous single 'La Isla Bonita' also used Spanish lyrics in the chorus.

A50. Pepsi used the song 'Like A Prayer' in its commercial advertising before the song was released. The supporting TV commercial showed Madonna drinking a can of Pepsi.

Here is a set of questions on films that Madonna has been involved with.

51. What was the first feature film Madonna appeared in?
    A. A Certain Sacrifice
    B. Bloodhounds of Broadway
    C. Desperately Seeking Susan
    D. Shanghai Surprise

52. How many feature films has Madonna appeared in as an actress?
    A. 12
    B. 22
    C. 32
    D. 42

53. Where was the movie Desperately Seeking Susan set?
    A. London
    B. Los Angeles
    C. New York City
    D. Paris

54. Who directed Madonna in Dick Tracy?
    A. Warren Beatty
    B. Tim Burton
    C. James Cameron
    D. Quentin Tarantino

55. What movie did Guy Ritchie direct with Madonna in a lead role?
- A. Agent Cody Banks
- B. Body Of Evidence
- C. Swept Away
- D. The Next Best Thing

56. Which movie did Madonna win a Golden Globe Award for best actress?
- A. Body of Evidence
- B. Dick Tracy
- C. Evita
- D. Shanghai Surprise

57. What was the name of the James Bond film Madonna sang the theme tune to?
- A. Casino Royale
- B. Die Another Day
- C. Quantum of Solace
- D. Tomorrow Never Dies

58. What was the name of the 1995 black comedy Madonna featured in?
- A. Foreclosure
- B. Forfeiture
- C. For Sure, For Sure
- D. Four Doors

59. Where was the movie Evita set?
- A. Algeria

B. Argentina
C. Aruba
D. Australia

60. How many times has Madonna won the Golden Raspberry Award for Worst Actress?
    A. 2
    B. 3
    C. 4
    D. 5

Here are the answers to the set of movie related questions.

A51. The first feature film Madonna appeared in was the 1979 film 'A Certain Sacrifice'. It was a low budget film, with most of the cast being unpaid. It was filmed from September 1979 until June 1981, but it was not released until 1985.

A52. According to Wikipedia, Madonna has appeared in a total of 27 feature films with 22 as an actress.

A53. The 1985 movie 'Desperately Seeking Susan' was set in New York City. Madonna co-starred with Rosanna Arquette.

A54. Warren Beatty directed the 1990 movie 'Dick Tracy'. Madonna played a character called Breathless Mahoney.

A55. Guy Ritchie directed Madonna as the lead actress in the 2002 movie 'Swept Away'. The film was not a commercial success.

A56. Madonna won Best Actress at the 1996 Golden Globe Awards for her starring role in the movie 'Evita'.

A57. Madonna performed the title song to 'Die Another Day'. She also had a cameo role in the movie, playing the part of a fencing instructor.

A58. Madonna featured in the 1995 black comedy 'Four Rooms' with an all star cast including Antonio Banderas, David Proval, Tim Roth, Quentin Tarantino and Bruce Willis amongst others.

A59. 'Evita' charted the story of Eva Peron who served as First Lady of Argentina from 1946 until her death from cancer in July 1952 aged just 33.

A60. Madonna has won the Golden Raspberry Award For Worst Actress a record five times.

Let's give you some easier questions.

61. What did Madonna say she wanted to do in her first TV interview in 1984?
    A. To rule the roost
    B. To rule the skies
    C. To rule the waves
    D. To rule the world

62. Which song includes the lyrics 'In the midnight hour, I can feel your power'?
    A. Cherish
    B. Express Yourself
    C. Like A Prayer
    D. Oh Father

63. Which song is dedicated to her daughter Lourdes?
    A. Bright Star
    B. Little Star
    C. Pole Star
    D. Superstar

64. What charity did she found in 1998?
    A. Rage Against The Machine
    B. Rainy Blues
    C. Raising Malawi
    D. Ray of Light Foundation

65. What was the name of the tour in support of the album Erotica?
- A. The Circus Show
- B. The Girlie Show
- C. The Sexy Show
- D. The Ultimate Show

66. Which of these actresses is not name-checked in the Vogue rap?
- A. Grace Kelly
- B. Marilyn Monroe
- C. Ginger Rogers
- D. Elizabeth Taylor

67. What was the opening track on the American Life album?
- A. American Life
- B. Nothing Fails
- C. Profusion
- D. Hollywood

68. Who did Madonna duet with on 'Love Song'?
- A. Bono
- B. Prince
- C. Sting
- D. Usher

69. Which supporting music video featured Madonna dressed in a red kimono, with a geisha inspired look?

A. La Isla Bonita
   B. Like A Virgin
   C. Material Girl
   D. Nothing Really Matters

70. Who provided background vocals on 'Take a Bow'?
   A. Babyface
   B. Snoop Dogg
   C. Lionel Richie
   D. Justin Timberlake

Here are the answers to the last set of questions.

A61. On her TV debut in 1984 on American Bandstand, she was asked by host Dick Clark, "What are your dreams?" Madonna replied, "To rule the world."

A62. The song Like a Prayer includes the lyrics 'In the midnight hour, I can feel your power'.

A63. 'Little Star' was dedicated entirely to her daughter Lourdes. The lyrics include "God gave a present to me; Made of flesh and bones; My life, my soul; You make my spirit whole."

A64. In 1996 Madonna founded Ray of Light Foundation, to promote peace, equal rights and education for all. Eight years later she founded Raising Malawi.

A65. The concert tour that was associated with the 'Erotica' album was known as The Girlie Show, and consisted of 39 shows from August 1993 to December 1993.

A66. Elizabeth Taylor is the odd one out who is not name-checked in the lyrics to 'Vogue'.

A67. 'American Life' was the first track on the 'American Life' album. It is a very powerful opening track, and its single release was a commercial success too.

A68. Madonna dueted with Prince on 'Love Song', a track on the 'Like a Prayer' album that Prince also co-wrote, co-performed and co-produced.

A69. Madonna dressed in a red kimono for the incredibly artistic video to support the 1999 single 'Nothing Really Matters'. Madonna declared that the inspiration for the video came from the novel 'Memoirs of a Geisha.'

A70. Babyface not only performed backing vocals on 'Take a Bow'; he also played synthesizer and co-produced the song.

Here is the next set of questions, let's hope you get most of them right.

71. How many MTV Music Awards has Madonna won?
    A. 11
    B. 14
    C. 17
    D. 20

72. Which song did Madonna sample Donna Summer's smash hit single 'I Feel Love'?
    A. Forbidden Love
    B. Future Lovers
    C. Justify My Love
    D. The Look Of Love

73. What was the name of the tour in support of the album Hard Candy?
    A. Sassy and Sweet
    B. Sticky and Sweet
    C. Sublime and Sweet
    D. Sugar and Sweet

74. Which album features the song 'Fever'?
    A. American Life
    B. Erotica
    C. Like A Virgin
    D. Rebel Heart

75. Which Italian city featured in the music video for 'Like a Virgin'?
    A. Florence
    B. Naples
    C. Rome
    D. Venice

76. How many singles were released from the album 'Like A Prayer'?
    A. 3
    B. 4
    C. 5
    D. 6

77. Who did Madonna famously insult in the documentary "Truth or Dare"?
    A. Alec Baldwin
    B. Nicholas Cage
    C. Kevin Costner
    D. Hugh Jackman

78. Who featured with Madonna on the single '4 Minutes'?
    A. Bruno Mars
    B. Harry Styles
    C. Justin Timberlake
    D. Timbaland

79. Which song includes the line 'I'm not your bitch, don't hang your shit on me'?

- A. American Life
- B. Cherish
- C. Express Yourself
- D. Human Nature

80. What was the name of the Broadway play Madonna starred in?
    - A. Speed The Blow
    - B. Speed The Flow
    - C. Speed The Plow
    - D. Speed The Slow

Here are the answers to the last set of questions.

A71. Madonna has won a total of 20 MTV Music Awards with her first coming in 1986. She has the second most number of awards of any artist.

A72. Madonna continually samples Donna Summer's 'I feel love' on 'Future Lovers', a track on the 'Confessions On A Dance Floor' album.

A73. The concert tour that was associated with the album Hard Candy was known as the Sticky and Sweet tour, and it consisted of 85 shows from August 2008 to September 2009.

A74. 'Fever' featured on the 1992 studio album 'Erotica'. It was one of six singles released from the album. The other singles were Erotica, Deep and Deeper, Bad Girl, Rain and Bye Bye Baby.

A75. The 'Like A Virgin' music video featured Madonna skipping around flirtatiously in Venice, and also dancing suggestively on a gondola.

A76. An incredible six singles were released from the 'Like A Prayer' album. They were, in chronological order, Like A Prayer, Express Yourself, Cherish, Oh Father, Dear Jessie and Keep it Together.

A77. Madonna made disparaging comments about Kevin Costner after he came to see her back stage during the Blond Ambition tours. It is believed her words stopped her becoming the leading actress role in The Bodyguard, a part that went to Whitney Houston.

A78. The single '4 Minutes' included vocals from both Justin Timberlake and Timbaland.

A79. The lyric 'I'm not your bitch, don't hang your shit on me' comes from her 2003 single 'Human Nature'. It's an R&B song and it was the fourth and final single from the 'Bedtime Stories' album.

A80. Speed The Plow was a 1988 production with Madonna in a leading role that ran for seven months on Broadway and a total of 279 performances.

Here is the next set of questions.

81. What musical instrument did Madonna play on every tour in the 2000s?
    A. Flute
    B. Guitar
    C. Piano
    D. Saxophone

82. Which of Madonna's singles is also the name of a Disney movie?
    A. Aladdin
    B. Cinderella
    C. Frozen
    D. Jungle Book

83. What is Madonna's only number one song in the Billboard Hot 100 during the 2000s?
    A. Don't Tell Me
    B. Hung Up
    C. Music
    D. Ray Of Light

84. What album was supported by the 2004 Re-Invention World Tour?
    A. American Life
    B. I'm Going To Tell You A Secret
    C. Rebel Heart
    D. Superpop

85. What fragrance did Madonna introduce in 2012?
    A. Dare To Dream
    B. I Double Dare You
    C. To Dare To Do
    D. Truth or Dare

86. Which album featured the song '4 Minutes'?
    A. American Life
    B. Hard Candy
    C. MDNA
    D. Rebel Heart

87. Where did Madonna move to in 2017?
    A. Andorra
    B. France
    C. Portugal
    D. Spain

88. What persona did Madonna wear an eye patch for?
    A. Madame Q
    B. Madame X
    C. Madame Y
    D. Madame Z

89. Which song did rappers Nicki Minaj and M.I.A. sing on?
    A. Girl Gone Wild
    B. Give Me All Your Luvin'

    C. Masterpiece
    D. Revolver

90. What is the official twitter account?
    A. @Madonna
    B. @MadonnaOfficial
    C. @OfficialMadonna
    D. @TheRealMadonna

Here are the answers to the last set of questions.

A81. Madonna has used a guitar on every tour throughout the 2000s.

A82. Madonna recorded 'Frozen' in 1998 and it features on the 'Ray of Light' album.

A83. Madonna's only US number 1 single during the 2000s is 'Music'. The song was inspired by a concert by Sting that Madonna attended in New York City.

A84. The Re-Invention World Tour was a 2004 tour in support of Madonna's 'American Life' studio album.

A85. Truth or Dare was the name of the fragrance launched in 2012 by Madonna. After the scent was developed, it was declared a modern interpretation of Madonna's mother's perfume. Truth or Dare includes essences from gardenia and tuberose, with jasmine, vanilla and musk all featuring too.

A86. '4 minutes' was on the 'Hard Candy' album. The album was a huge commercial success and debuted at number-one in over thirty countries.

A87. Madonna moved to Portugal in the summer of 2017. Many celebrities threatened to leave the USA if Donald Trump was elected as president, but Madonna actually did.

A88. Madonna wears an eye patch for her persona 'Madame X' explaining, "She sleeps with one eye open. And she travels through the day with one eye shut."

A89. Rappers Nicki Minaj and M.I.A. performed guest vocals on 'Give Me All Your Luvin'' which was a single taken from the 'MDNA' album.

A90. @Madonna is the official twitter account. It was set up in March 2012 and it has over three million followers.

Here is the final set of questions. Enjoy.

91. Who did Madonna dedicate 'Papa Don't Preach' to?
    A. Eddie Murphy
    B. Hulk Hogan
    C. Ronald Reagan
    D. The Pope

92. What album featured the single 'Vogue'?
    A. Erotica
    B. I'm Breathless
    C. Like a Prayer
    D. You Can Dance

93. How many records has Madonna sold?
    A. Over 100 Million
    B. Over 200 million
    C. Over 300 million
    D. Over 400 million

94. What was the most successful single from the 'Confessions On A Dance Floor' album?
    A. Get Together
    B. Hung Up
    C. Jump
    D. Sorry

95. Which song starts with the line 'Life is a mystery; everyone must stand alone'?

A. Cherish
   B. Like A Prayer
   C. Live To Tell
   D. True Blue

96. What is the title of an illustrated children's book Madonna published in 2003?
   A. The Irish Dancers
   B. The English Roses
   C. The Scottish Warriors
   D. The Welsh Dragons

97. How did Madonna break her collarbone in 2005?
   A. Fell off a horse
   B. Fell off a hotel balcony
   C. Fell off a ladder
   D. Fell off stage

98. Where did Madonna dream of in 'La Isla Bonita'?
   A. San Antonio
   B. San Diego
   C. San Jose
   D. San Pedro

99. Which music video featured Madonna's dog Chiquita?
   A. Cherish
   B. Express Yourself

    C. Human Nature
    D. La Isla Bonita

100. Who were the support act on Madonna's first tour?
    A. Boyz II Men
    B. New Kids On The Block
    C. The Beastie Boys
    D. Level 42

101. What is Madonna's best selling song worldwide?
    A. 4 Minutes
    B. Hung Up
    C. Like A Prayer
    D. Like A Virgin

Here are the final set of answers.

A91. Madonna dedicated 'Papa Don't Preach' to Pope John Paul II, who had urged people to boycott her concerts, partly due to the song's lyrics about teenage pregnancy and abortion.

A92. 'Vogue' was featured on the album 'I'm Breathless'. The whole album was recorded in just three weeks.

A93. Madonna has sold well over 300 million records worldwide.

A94. The best selling song on the 'Confessions on a Dance Floor' album was 'Hung Up' which sold over 5 million copies and went on to top the charts in 41 countries.

A95. 'Like a Prayer' starts with 'Life is a mystery, everyone must stand alone, I hear you call my name, and it feels like home'.

A96. The English Roses is an illustrated children's book that was published in 2003. It tells the story of the envy and jealousy of four schoolgirls. It became the fastest selling children's picture book of all time and went on to sell over a million copies worldwide. Madonna donated all the proceeds from the book to a children's charity.

A97. In August 2005, Madonna broke her collarbone, a hand, and cracked three ribs after falling off a horse.

A98. The opening lyrics to 'La Isla Bonita' are 'Last night I dreamt of San Pedro, just like I'd never gone, I knew the song, a young girl with eyes like the desert, it all seems like yesterday, not far away.'

A99. The music video for 'Human Nature' featuring Chiquita and Madonna clad in skintight leather outfits was shot in two days in May 1995.

A100. The Beastie Boys were the support act for Madonna's first tour – The Virgin Tour, for which Madonna designed all the costumes.

A101. A controversial answer to finish with, as record sales are so fragmented; however, it is widely acknowledged by industry sources, official charts and Wikipedia that Madonna's best selling single of all time worldwide – pure sales - is 'Like A Virgin.'

That's it. I hope you enjoyed this book, and I hope you got most of the answers right. I also hope you learnt a few new things about the incredible woman and musician that is Madonna.

support@glowwormpress.com is the email address if you saw anything wrong, or you have any comments or suggestions. I do read all messages sent in, and this book has already been updated because of messages left by others.

Thanks for reading, and if you did enjoy the book, please leave a positive review on Amazon.

Printed in Great Britain
by Amazon

54160557R00036